Investing with Insight: The Peter Lynch Story

Peter Lynch, born on January 19, 1944, in Newton, Massachusetts, grew up in a modest family. His father passed away when Peter was just ten years old, significantly impacting his early life and his family's financial situation. Lynch helped his mother financially by caddying at the Brae Burn Country Club starting at age 11. It was there that he overheard discussions about the stock market from the wealthy businessmen he caddied for, sparking his interest in investments and laying the groundwork for his future career.

Lynch attended Boston College, where he studied history, psychology, and philosophy, graduating in 1965. During these years, he made his first investment in Flying Tiger Airlines, a cargo airline company. This investment increased in value by more than 1000%, allowing him to pay for his college tuition and solidifying his interest in the stock market.

Early Career and Joining Fidelity Investments

During his time as a caddy, he had the opportunity to caddy for Fidelity's president, which helped him secure an internship at Fidelity Investments. In 1966, before completing his MBA, Lynch started his career as an intern at Fidelity Investments. After earning his MBA from Wharton in 1968, he returned to Fidelity as a full-time employee. He began as an investment analyst, covering the textiles, mining, and metals industries. Lynch quickly made a name for himself with his keen analytical skills and ability to identify promising investment opportunities.

Lynch's hard work and impressive performance did not go unnoticed. In 1977, at the age of 33, he was appointed head of the newly established Fidelity Magellan Fund. At the time, the Magellan Fund was a small and relatively unknown mutual fund with assets of about $18 million. Lynch's management style and investment strategy would soon change that.

Investment Philosophy and Strategy

Peter Lynch's investment philosophy was both simple and revolutionary. He believed in doing thorough research and investing in what he knew and understood. He often emphasized the importance of "investing in what you know" and finding growth opportunities in companies and industries familiar to the investor. Lynch was also a strong advocate for individual stock picking and was known for his bottom-up approach to investing, which focuses on analyzing individual companies rather than relying on market trends or economic forecasts. This method involves a detailed examination of a company's fundamentals, such as its financial statements, products, management, and competitive position, to determine its potential for growth and profitability. By focusing more on the intrinsic value of a company (and comparatively less on macroeconomics and market cycles), Lynch believed investors could uncover hidden gems that were often overlooked by others.

Lynch also coined the term "tenbagger" to describe investments that appreciated tenfold or more. His ability to identify such stocks became a hallmark of his investment strategy. He often looked for undervalued companies with strong growth potential, solid fundamentals, and competent management teams.

Some of his most famous "tenbaggers" included Dunkin' Donuts, which he purchased when it was a regional chain and saw grow into a national brand, and Ford Motor Company, which he invested in during a turnaround period, leading to significant gains. These examples demonstrate Lynch's keen eye for spotting companies with the potential for explosive growth.

Turning the Magellan Fund into a Powerhouse

Under Lynch's leadership, the Magellan Fund grew exponentially. From 1977 to 1990, the fund's assets skyrocketed from $18 million to over $14 billion. Lynch's performance was nothing short of extraordinary, achieving an average annual return of 29% during his tenure. This remarkable track record earned him widespread acclaim and established him as one of the greatest investors of all time.

Lynch's success was not without its challenges. The stock market experienced significant volatility during his tenure, including the bear market of the early 1980s and the crash of 1987. However, Lynch's disciplined approach and his ability to stay focused on his long-term strategy helped him navigate these turbulent times and deliver outstanding returns to his investors.

In 1990, at the peak of his career, Peter Lynch shocked the investment world by announcing his retirement from the Magellan Fund. At just 46 years old, Lynch chose to step away from the high-pressure world of fund management to spend more time with his family. His departure marked the end of an era for Fidelity Investments and the Magellan Fund, but his influence on the world of investing continued to be felt.

Life After Retirement

Despite retiring from active fund management, Peter Lynch remained deeply involved in the financial world. He continued to work with Fidelity Investments as a research consultant, offering his expertise and insights to the next generation of fund managers. Lynch also dedicated significant time to philanthropy, supporting various educational and medical causes through the Lynch Foundation, which he established with his wife, Carolyn.

Peter Lynch is also well-known for his contributions to investment literature. He authored several best-selling books aimed at demystifying the world of investing for the general public. His most famous work, "One Up on Wall Street," published in 1989, became an instant classic. In it, Lynch shares his investment philosophy, strategies, and personal anecdotes, offering valuable lessons to both novice and experienced investors.

Following "One Up on Wall Street," Lynch wrote "Beating the Street" in 1993, where he provided a detailed look at his stock-picking strategies and the success stories behind his investments. He also co-authored "Learn to Earn" in 1995, a book designed to educate young people about the basics of investing and the stock market.

Through his books, Peter Lynch emphasized the importance of thorough research, patience, and investing in what one knows. His approachable writing style and practical advice made his books popular among a wide audience and cemented his legacy as a great educator in the field of finance.

Investment Legacy and Philosophy

Peter Lynch's investment philosophy continues to influence investors worldwide. His belief in conducting in-depth research, understanding the companies in which one invests, and focusing on long-term growth has become a cornerstone of modern investment strategy. Lynch's approach to identifying and investing in "tenbaggers" and his emphasis on individual stock picking have inspired countless investors to take a more hands-on approach to their portfolios.

Lynch also popularized the concept of the Price-Earnings (P/E) ratio as a critical tool for evaluating stocks. He believed that by comparing a company's P/E ratio to its growth rate (PEG ratio), investors could better assess its value and growth potential. This method remains a fundamental analysis technique used by investors today.

Throughout his career and into his retirement, Peter Lynch has been known for his humility and down-to-earth personality. Despite his immense success, he remained accessible and committed to helping others achieve their financial goals. His work with the Lynch Foundation and his efforts to educate the public about investing reflect his enduring commitment to giving back to society.

Even years after his retirement, Lynch's insights and strategies remain relevant and are frequently cited by financial professionals and individual investors alike. His ability to simplify complex investment concepts and his track record of success have made him a timeless figure in the world of finance.

Peter Lynch's Most Notable Investments During His Time at the Magellan Fund

DUNKIN' DONUTS: Lynch invested in Dunkin' Donuts when it was primarily a regional chain. As a customer, he first appreciated their high-quality coffee, which sparked his interest in the brand. Recognizing the company's strong identity and emphasis on quality coffee and baked goods, he conducted further analysis. Lynch believed that as consumer interest in coffee culture grew, Dunkin' would benefit significantly from expansion. His insights proved correct, as the stock appreciated substantially as the company opened new locations and increased its national presence.

GENERAL ELECTRIC (GE: Lynch invested in GE due to its status as a diversified conglomerate with a strong leadership team, particularly under CEO Jack Welch. He admired GE's focus on innovation and operational efficiency across various sectors, including energy, healthcare, and finance. Lynch believed that GE's robust growth prospects and commitment to shareholder value made it a solid investment.

FANNIE MAE: The Federal National Mortgage Association, commonly known as Fannie Mae, is a government-sponsored enterprise (GSE) established to enhance the liquidity of the mortgage market. Its primary function is to buy mortgage loans from lenders, providing them with capital to issue new loans, thereby supporting homeownership and affordable housing in the United States. Lynch invested in Fannie Mae, appreciating its crucial role in the U.S. housing finance system.

The company's government-backed securities offered a level of security and stability, making it an attractive investment during times of economic uncertainty. Lynch's foresight in recognizing the importance of Fannie Mae's business model allowed him to capitalize on significant returns as housing markets boomed.

PHILIP MORRIS: Lynch saw potential in Philip Morris, the parent company of well-known cigarette brands such as Marlboro, Virginia Slims, and Parliament. Despite the regulatory challenges facing the tobacco industry, he recognized the company's strong cash flow, dominant market position, and ability to adapt to changing regulations. Lynch believed that Philip Morris could continue to generate substantial profits, especially as the company diversified its product offerings and expanded into international markets. This global expansion allowed Philip Morris to tap into emerging markets, increasing its revenue streams and mitigating risks associated with domestic regulations.

FORD MOTOR COMPANY: Lynch saw potential in Ford during a critical turnaround period. The company was restructuring its operations and refocusing on its core automotive business. Lynch's research indicated that Ford had strong brand equity and innovative product offerings. Between 1982 and 1988, Ford's shares increased from $4 to $38 as the company's restructuring efforts began to show results, leading to increased profitability and stock price appreciation. His investment paid off, demonstrating Lynch's keen eye for identifying companies poised for significant growth.

MCDONALD'S: Lynch recognized McDonald's as a leader in the fast-food industry, with a strong global brand and a proven business model. He was particularly impressed by the company's ability to adapt its menu to local tastes and preferences, which facilitated its international expansion. His investment in McDonald's yielded impressive returns as the company continued to grow and innovate, maintaining its competitive edge in the fast-food market.

MCI: Lynch invested in MCI, a telecommunications company that was a key player in the market alongside AT&T. He recognized the potential for growth in the telecommunications sector, especially following the deregulation of the industry in the 1980s, which included the significant breakup of AT&T in 1982. This breakup opened the market to competition, allowing MCI to offer innovative services and competitive pricing. As a result, MCI was able to gain significant market share, leading to substantial stock appreciation.

GENERAL PUBLIC UTILITIES (GPU): Lynch invested in General Public Utilities, a utility company that provided electricity and gas services to customers in the northeastern United States. At the time, GPU faced regulatory challenges that affected its operations and profitability. However, Lynch believed that the company's underlying fundamentals, including its stable revenue stream and essential services, combined with the overall stability of the utility sector, would lead to long-term growth. As regulatory issues were resolved, GPU experienced a rebound in stock performance, reflecting Lynch's confidence in the company's potential.

VOLVO: Lynch saw value in Volvo, known for its reputation for safety and quality in the automotive market. He believed that Volvo's strong brand and focus on innovation, particularly in safety features, positioned it well for growth. At the time, Lynch personally drove a Volvo and referred to it as his favorite stock to hold. His investment paid off as the company expanded its product offerings and strengthened its market presence.

STUDENT LOAN MARKETING ASSOCIATION (Sallie Mae): Lynch recognized the importance of the Student Loan Marketing Association in the U.S. education finance system. With the increasing demand for higher education and student loans, Lynch saw significant growth potential. His investment was rewarded as Sallie Mae benefited from the expanding student loan market.

KEMPER: Lynch invested in Kemper, a financial services company involved in insurance and asset management. He appreciated Kemper's strong market position and its ability to generate consistent cash flow. The company's diversified offerings and management's focus on profitability contributed to its stock's growth during Lynch's investment period.

LOWE'S: Lynch recognized Lowe's potential as a leading home improvement retailer. He believed in the company's strong brand and ability to capture market share from competitors like Home Depot. With the increasing trend of home improvement projects among consumers, Lowe's stock appreciated significantly as the company expanded its store footprint and enhanced its product offerings.

Your ultimate success or failure will depend on your ability to ignore the worries of the world long enough to allow your investments to succeed.

If you can follow only one bit of data, follow the earnings – assuming the company in question has earnings. I subscribe to the crusty notion that sooner or later earnings make or break an investment in equities. What the stock price does today, tomorrow, or next week is only a distraction.

When you start to confuse Freddie Mac, Sallie Mae and Fannie Mae with members of your family, and you remember 2,000 stock symbols but forget the children's birthdays, there's a good chance you've become too wrapped up in your work.

As I look back on it now, it's obvious that studying history and philosophy was much better preparation for the stock market than, say, studying statistics.

During the Gold Rush, most would-be miners lost money, but people who sold them picks, shovels, tents and blue-jeans (Levi Strauss) made a nice profit.

Thousands of experts study overbought indicators, oversold indicators, head-and-shoulder patterns, put-call ratios, the Fed's policy on money supply, foreign investment, the movement of the constellations through the heavens, and the moss on oak trees, and they can't predict markets with any useful consistency, any more than the gizzard squeezers could tell the Roman emperors when the Huns would attack.

If Coca-Cola has a P/E ratio of 15, it's reasonable to expect the company to grow at around 15 percent annually. However, if the P/E ratio is lower than the growth rate, you might have found a bargain. For example, a company growing at 12 percent per year with a P/E ratio of 6 is a very appealing investment.

Never invest in any idea you can't illustrate with a crayon

Time is on your side when you own shares of superior companies.

Never invest in a company without understanding its finances. The biggest losses in stocks come from companies with poor balance sheets.

Everyone has the brainpower to make money in stocks. Not everyone has the stomach. If you are susceptible to selling everything in a panic, you ought to avoid stocks and mutual funds altogether.

If you're lucky enough to have been rewarded in life to the degree that I have, there comes a point at which you have to decide whether to become a slave to your net worth by devoting the rest of your life to increasing it or to let what you've accumulated begin to serve you.

There's no shame in losing money on a stock. Everybody does it. What is shameful is to hold on to a stock, or worse, to buy more of it when the fundamentals are deteriorating.

I think you have to learn that there's a company behind every stock, and that there's only one real reason why stocks go up. Companies go from doing poorly to doing well or small companies grow to large companies.

The Rule of 72 is useful in determining how fast money will grow. Take the annual return from any investment, expressed as a percentage, and divide it into 72. The result is the number of years it will take to double your money.

I deal in facts, not forecasting the future. That's crystal ball stuff. That doesn't work.

When stocks are attractive, you buy them. Sure, they can go lower. I've bought stocks at $12 that went to $2, but then they later went to $30. You just don't know when you can find the bottom.

Investing $100,000 in stocks on July 1, 1994, and keeping it invested for five years would have grown to $341,722. Missing just the top thirty days, however, would leave you with only $153,792. This shows the value of staying invested, despite the possibility of an overvalued market.

Although it's easy to forget sometimes, a share of stock is not a lottery ticket. It's part ownership of a business.

There are substantial rewards for adopting a regular routine of investing and following it no matter what, and additional rewards for buying more shares when most investors are scared into selling.

Investing in stocks is an art, not a science, and people who've been trained to rigidly quantify everything have a big disadvantage.

Invest in simple companies that appear dull, mundane, out of favor, and haven't caught the fancy of Wall Street.

Diversifying into unknown companies just to mix things up isn't wise. This kind of diversity is often a trap for small investors. However, putting all your money into one stock isn't safe either because unexpected events can negatively affect it. For smaller portfolios, owning three to ten stocks is a balanced approach.

You shouldn't just pick a stock – you should do your homework.

Behind every stock is a company. Find out what it's doing.

My high-tech aversion caused me to make fun of the typical biotech enterprise: $100 million in cash from selling shares, one hundred Ph.D.'s, 99 microscopes, and zero revenues.

Equity mutual funds are the perfect solution for people who want to own stocks without doing their own research.

To me, an investment is simply a gamble in which you've managed to tilt the odds in your favor.

In the investment world, being good means getting it right six times out of ten. Expecting to be right nine times out of ten is unrealistic. This isn't like pure science where you find a clear answer; by the time you have an "Aha" moment, stocks like Chrysler or Boeing could have already quadrupled. You must be willing to take some risks.

The extravagance of any corporate office is directly proportional to management's reluctance to reward the shareholders.

Far more money has been lost by investors preparing for corrections, or trying to anticipate corrections, than has been lost in corrections themselves.

A person who owns property and has a stake in the enterprise is likely to work harder and feel happier and do a better job than a person who doesn't.

You can find good reasons to scuttle your equities in every morning paper and on every broadcast of the nightly news.

People who want to know how stocks fared on any given day ask, "Where did the Dow close?" I'm more interested in how many stocks went up versus how many went down. These so-called advance/decline numbers paint a more realistic picture.

Once I've established the size of the company relative to others in a particular industry, next I place it into one of six general categories: slow growers, stalwarts, fast growers, cyclicals, asset plays, and turnarounds... By putting your stocks into categories you'll have a better idea of what to expect from them.

Twenty years in this business convinces me that any normal person using the customary three percent of the brain can pick stocks just as well, if not better, than the average Wall Street expert.

When an Internet company I favor is priced at $30 a share, and yours at $10, price-focused individuals might think mine is superior. This is a misconception. The current market price doesn't reveal which company will succeed in the next few years.

If you're considering a stock on the strength of some specific product that a company makes, the first thing to find out is: What effect will the success of the product have on the company's bottom line?

When management owns stock, then rewarding the shareholders becomes a first priority, whereas when management simply collects a paycheck, then increasing salaries becomes a first priority.

I talk to hundreds of companies a year and spend hour after hour in heady pow-wows with CEOs, financial analysts and my colleagues in the mutual-fund business, but I stumble onto the big winners in extracurricular situations, the same way you do.

A dip in the price of a good stock is only a setback if you sell at that price and don't reinvest. To me, a price drop is a chance to buy more of your underperformers and promising laggards.

If you can't convince yourself "When I'm down 25 percent, I'm a buyer" and avoid the fatal thought "When I'm down 25 percent, I'm a seller," you'll never make significant gains in the stock market.

In the long run, it's not just how much money you make that will determine your future prosperity. It's how much of that money you put to work by saving it and investing it.

I'm always fully invested. It's a great feeling to be caught with your pants up.

A stock market decline is as routine as a January blizzard in Colorado. If you're prepared, it can't hurt you. A decline is a great opportunity to pick up the bargains left behind by investors who are fleeing the storm in panic.

The trick is not to learn to trust your gut feelings, but rather to discipline yourself to ignore them. Stand by your stocks as long as the fundamental story of the company hasn't changed.

Long shots almost always miss the mark.

Look for companies that consistently buy back their own shares.

Carefully consider the price-earnings ratio. If the stock is grossly overpriced, even if everything else goes right, you won't make any money.

I always thought if you looked at ten companies, you'd find one that's interesting, if you'd look at 20, you'd find two, or if you look at hundred you'll find ten. The person that turns over the most rocks wins the game. And that's always been my philosophy.

Understand the nature of the companies you own and the specific reasons for holding the stock. ("It is really going up!" doesn't count.)

If you hope to have more money tomorrow than you have today, you've got to put a chunk of your assets into stocks. Sooner or later, a portfolio of stocks or stock mutual funds will turn out to be a lot more valuable than a portfolio of bonds or CDs or money-market funds.

If you can find a company that can get away with raising prices year after year without losing customers (an addictive product such as cigarettes fills the bill), you've got a terrific investment.

If you're prepared to invest in a company, then you ought to be able to explain why in simple language that a fifth grader could understand, and quickly enough so the fifth grader won't get bored.

Absent a lot of surprises, stocks are relatively predictable over twenty years.
As to whether they're going to be higher or lower in two to three years, you might as well flip a coin to decide.

The biggest winners are surprises to me, and takeovers are even more surprising. It takes years, not months, to produce big results.

The list of qualities (an investor should have) include patience, self-reliance, common sense, a tolerance for pain, open-mindedness, detachment, persistence, humility, flexibility, a willingness to do independent research, an equal willingness to admit mistakes, and the ability to ignore general panic.

There are five basic ways a company can increase earnings: reduce costs; raise prices; expand into new markets; sell more of its product in the old markets; or revitalize, close, or otherwise dispose of a losing operation.

All the math you need in the stock market you get in the fourth grade.

The best stock to buy is the one you already own.

I'm always on the lookout for great companies in lousy industries. A great industry that's growing fast, such as computers or medical technology, attracts too much attention and too many competitors.

To all the dozens of lessons we're supposed to have learned...I can add three:

(1) don't let nuisances ruin a good portfolio;

(2) don't let nuisances ruin a good vacation; and

(3) never travel abroad when you're light on cash.

Understanding a company's story is much easier if you grasp the basics of its business. That's why I prefer investing in simple businesses like panty hose or motel chains over complex ones like satellites or fiber optics. The simpler, the better. When I hear, "Any idiot could run this company," I take it as a good sign, because eventually, an idiot likely will.

My diaries are full of such missed opportunities, but the stock market is merciful—it always gives the nincompoop a second chance.

Moderately
fast growers
(20 to 25 percent)
in non-growth
industries are
ideal investments.

It's human nature to keep doing something as long as it's pleasurable and you can succeed at it, which is why the world population continues to double every 40 years.

While catching up on the news is merely depressing to the citizen who has no stocks, it is a dangerous habit for the investor.

There's lots of stocks out there and all you need is a few of 'em. So that's been my philosophy. You have to let the big ones make up for your mistakes.

The junior high schools and high schools of America have forgotten to teach one of the most important courses of all. Investing.

All you need for a lifetime of successful investing is a few big winners, and the pluses from those will overwhelm the minuses from the stocks that don't work out.

In stocks as in romance, ease of divorce is not a sound basis for commitment.

I can't recall ever once having seen the name of a market timer on Forbes' annual list of the richest people in the world. If it were truly possible to predict corrections, you'd think somebody would have made billions by doing it.

Even the dentist has three or four tips, and in the next few days I look up his recommendations in the newspaper and they've all gone up. When the neighbors tell me what to buy, and then I wish I had taken their advice, it's a sure sign that the market has reached a top and is due for a tumble.

Owning stocks is like having children – don't get involved with more than you can handle.

There is frequently a disconnect between how a company's operations perform and how its stock performs over months or even years. Yet, over time, the success of the company and its stock are completely correlated. Understanding this gap is essential for making profits; being patient and investing in successful companies pays off.

The worst thing you can do is invest in companies you know nothing about. Unfortunately, buying stocks on ignorance is still a popular American pastime.

There seems to be an unwritten rule on Wall Street: If you don't understand it, then put your life savings into it. Shun the enterprise around the corner, which can at least be observed, and seek out the one that manufactures an incomprehensible product.

The simpler it is,
the better I like it.

When you sell in
desperation, you
always sell cheap.

You have to keep your priorities straight if you plan to do well in stocks.

Find something you enjoy doing and give it everything you've got, and the money will take care of itself.

There is always something to worry about. Avoid weekend thinking and ignoring the latest dire predictions of the newscasters. Sell a stock because the company's fundamentals deteriorate, not because the sky is falling.

The real key to making money in stocks is not to get scared out of them.

Bargains are the holy grail of the true stockpicker. The fact that 10 to 30 percent of our net worth is lost in a market sell-off is of little consequence. We see the latest correction not as a disaster but as an opportunity to acquire more shares at low prices. This is how great fortunes are made over time.

The S&P is up 343.8 percent for 10 years. That is a four-bagger. The general equity funds are up 283 percent. So it's getting worse, the deterioration by professionals is getting worse. The public would be better off in an index fund.

Nobody predicted the dire economic situation in 1982, with 14% inflation, 12% unemployment, and a 20% prime rate, marking the worst recession since the Depression. It took everyone by surprise. That's why I don't worry about economic predictions. I've always said if you spend 13 minutes a year on economics, you've wasted 10 minutes.

Know what you own, and know why you own it.

Hold no more stocks than you can remain informed on.

Visiting stores and testing products is one of the critical elements of the analyst's job.

When people discover they are no good at baseball or hockey, they put away their bats and their skates and they take up amateur golf or stamp collecting or gardening. But when people discover they are no good at picking stocks, they are likely to continue to do it anyway.

Nobody can predict interest rates, the future direction of the economy or the stock market. Dismiss all such forecasts and concentrate on what's actually happening to the companies in which you've invested.

In the long run, a portfolio of well chosen stocks and/or equity mutual funds will always outperform a portfolio of bonds or a money-market account. In the long run, a portfolio of poorly chosen stocks won't outperform the money left under the mattress.

The typical big winner in the Lynch portfolio (I continue to pick my share of losers, too!) generally takes three to ten years or more to play out.

In our society, it's been the men who've handled most of the finances, and the women who've stood by and watched men botch things up.

If you can't find any companies that you think are attractive, put your money in the bank until you discover some.

The study of logic has greatly aided my stock selection by highlighting Wall Street's illogical tendencies. Like the early Greeks who endlessly debated a horse's teeth count without inspection, many investors predict stock prices without researching the companies.

It would be wonderful if we could avoid the setbacks with timely exits, but nobody has figured out how to predict them.

Long-term investing has gotten so popular, it's easier to admit you're a crack addict than to admit you're a short-term investor.

If a picture is worth a thousand words, in business, so is a number.

When even the analysts are bored, it's time to start buying.

To my mind, the stock price is the least useful information you can track, and it's the most widely tracked.

I've always said, the key organ here isn't the brain, it's the stomach. When things start to decline – there are bad headlines in the papers and on television – will you have the stomach for the market volatility and the broad-based pessimism that tends to come with it?

The stock market really isn't a gamble, as long as you pick good companies that you think will do well, and not just because of the stock price.

The basic story remains simple and never-ending. Stocks aren't lottery tickets. There's a company attached to every share.

By the way, the odds against making a living in the day-trading business are about the same as the odds against making a living at racetracks, blackjack tables, or video poker.

By now, you might question the logic of investing in an old company like IBM, GM, or U.S. Steel. There are a few key reasons. Big companies are typically safer and unlikely to go bankrupt. They often pay dividends and hold valuable assets that can be sold for profit.